THE ART AND SCIENCE
OF
SELLING YOUR BUSINESS

A PRACTICAL GUIDE
BY ACCOMPLISHED BUSINESS ATTORNEYS

Raymond E. Saunders and David L. Reich

of the Law Firm of

Lawrence, Kamin, Saunders & Uhlenhop, LLC

ISBN-13: 978-1493580972
ISBN-10: 1493580973

TABLE OF CONTENTS

A Word from the Authors

Although we have acted as counsel, sometimes for the purchaser and sometimes for the seller, in what we estimate as more than 400 transactions, it might never have occurred to us that we should write a book covering this subject. The inspiration and motivation for writing this book came from Gary Klaben of Coyle Financial Counsel, Inc. He predicted that it would be easy and enjoyable and that we would advance our knowledge by doing so. In every respect he was correct. It was a lot of fun, and we have a feeling of accomplishment. We are grateful to Gary, and to our partner Joe Zarlengo for introducing Gary to us.

Other partners in our law firm, Bob Schlossberg and Mitch Goldberg, were very helpful in providing meaningful suggestions and editorial assistance.

We owe a special thank-you to our assistant, Elizabeth Szklarz, who laboriously typed and retyped the drafts that finally evolved into this book. Our longtime assistant, Anna Strelka, an excellent author and grammarian in her own right, edited this work and made numerous beneficial suggestions that we have incorporated.

The next pages will describe the proud authors of this book.

Raymond E. Saunders

For more than 50 years, clients have counted Raymond E. Saunders among their most trusted advisors, not just in law, but in all aspects of their business.

Ray specializes in corporate structure, business transactions, income tax, mergers and acquisitions, trusts and estate and gift tax (including cross-generational transfer and ownership of business). Technically proficient as a lawyer and a Certified Public Accountant, his special strength is his pragmatic approach and ability to craft simple solutions to complex problems. He has developed the skill of being able to provide concise and simple oral and written explanations of complex legal and business matters.

The partners of Lawrence, Kamin, Saunders & Uhlenhop have such respect for Ray's sound business judgment that they chose Ray to manage the firm's business decisions. For more than 20 years, Ray acted as the sole managing partner of the firm. He established most of the procedures and practices that currently are being followed by the firm. As one of his longtime partners once summarized, Ray "is an incredibly capable lawyer who, in the course of handling the multitude of details involved in a legal matter, never loses sight of the important business issues."

Ray enjoys traveling both domestically and abroad with his wife Inez. As a senior partner of the firm, Ray enjoys working with and supervising other attorneys. However, he so enjoys the practice of law that he wants to be immersed in the decisions that are important to clients.

Contact Information

Raymond E. Saunders, Partner

Lawrence, Kamin, Saunders & Uhlenhop, LLC
300 South Wacker Drive, Suite 500
Chicago, IL 60606

Phone: 312-924-4243

Email: resaunders@LKSU.com

Website: www.LKSU.com

Practice Areas
Income Tax
Estate and Gift Tax
Mergers and Acquisitions

Experience
Lawrence, Kamin, Saunders & Uhlenhop, LLC
  Partner: 1962-Present
  Managing Partner: 1985-2005

Education
Northwestern University Law School, J.D.,
  cum laude, 1956
  Order of the Coif
  Editor, *Northwestern University Law Review*
Northwestern University, B.S., Accounting,
  cum laude, 1953

Honors
Illinois Silver Medal, 1954 CPA Examination
  - second-highest grade in Illinois
Elijah Watt Sells Award, 1954 CPA
  Examination – top ten highest grades in
  United States

Bar Admissions
State of Illinois

**Professional Memberships
& Affiliations**
Chicago Bar Association

David L. Reich

Since joining Lawrence, Kamin, Saunders & Uhlenhop in 1991, David L. Reich has represented countless clients in transactional matters, including purchases and sales of businesses, commercial and industrial real estate transactions, leasing, and real estate lending on behalf of lenders and borrowers. David is also a specialist in estate and gift tax planning and estate and trust administration, business succession planning, and general corporate and business transactions and contracts.

David is an active board member for several charitable organizations and enjoys spending time with his family, traveling, running, playing golf and skiing.

Contact Information
David L. Reich, Partner
Lawrence, Kamin, Saunders & Uhlenhop, LLC
300 South Wacker Drive, Suite 500
Chicago, IL 60606
   Phone: 312-924-4246
   Email: dreich@LKSU.com
   Website: www.LKSU.com

Practice Areas
Businesses & Corporations
Estate Planning
Real Estate

Experience
Lawrence, Kamin, Saunders & Uhlenhop, LLC
Partner: 1998-Present
Associate: 1991-1998

Education
Northwestern University Law School, J.D., 1991
Indiana University, B.S., Finance, 1985

Bar Admissions
State of Illinois

Court Admissions
United States District Courts
Northern District of Illinois

Professional Memberships
& Affiliations
Chicago Bar Association
Israel Cancer Research Fund
 Board of Directors
Modestus Bauer Foundation
 Board of Directors
Highland Park Community Foundation
 Board of Directors

INTRODUCTION

This book is not directed to those who throughout their business career will buy and sell businesses many times. This is for an owner who has built or inherited his business, and has never sold a business.

Selling a business is both an art and a science.

In the following pages we will offer you not only the benefit of our technical legal expertise, but insights into the subtler and more intuitive aspects of the selling process that we have acquired over many years of experience representing both buyers and sellers.

As a business owner, you have undoubtedly acquired both a thorough grasp of the technical details of running your business and a capacity for intuitive judgment in business matters. Both will come into play during the selling process.

Although you will employ professionals, your role is very important:

- You should guide and not merely follow.

- You should be prepared, after weighing and considering advice, to make the necessary decisions.

- You will need a good understanding of the steps and procedures involved in selling a business in order to communicate with others, e.g., spouse, children, employees, customers, and vendors.

This is probably the most important single decision of your business life. Do not proceed without adequate preparation.

How To Prepare

- Read this book carefully and reflect on points raised.

- Read other books as well.

- Talk to friends and business associates who have gone through the process.

- Formulate the questions that you need to answer.

The decision to sell is the first and most important step in the process. Self reflection and analysis are necessary to make the right choice for you. Chapter 1 of this book offers suggestions that might be helpful to you in making this decision.

CHAPTER 1

The Decision to Sell - Personal Aspects

The personal aspects of selling your business may actually be more important than the financial ones, so consider these first.

Start with an analysis of your age and life style. There is no age that is the benchmark for sale and retirement. Some individuals are ready in their mid-50's or earlier. Others want to die at their desk in the office.

Consider whether you really should sell. Do you have children who can succeed you in running the business? Are there key employees who can take over and run the business?

Analyze what you will do with your time if you retire. If you stay around your house, your spouse is likely to develop a list of tasks that you might not find to your liking. If you are an avid golfer you will probably enjoy retirement, since golf can occupy most of the day. The same is true if you like to putter around and fix things in your house.

However, many active, energetic business people are bored after a sale. They miss the day-to-day stimulation and pressures. They miss the ego gratification that stems from the respect given to them by their employees and vendors. When a business owner says "Jump," people frequently say "How high?" You might just miss this adulation.

Also, consider your mental health. It is not uncommon for an individual to witness the onset of dementia or at least some slowing of mental function following the sale of a business.

Will you have regrets? There are countless examples of individuals who end up attempting to repurchase their business. It is common for an entrepreneur who has built a business to be critical of the practices of his purchaser, sometimes justifiably, sometimes not.

On the other hand, maybe you are just tired of the day-to-day grind and need to do something different.

This is a major life decision. You may wish to consult a mental health professional to assist in analyzing the individual issues involved in deciding whether or not you should sell.

Most people will follow their customary methods of making difficult decisions. Some do this by making a list of the pros and cons; others by following their intuition.

Unfortunately, this decision is one that must be made without knowing many of the crucial details. Will the purchaser want you to stay involved for a period of time? How much money will you receive, and will this be sufficient to support your lifestyle for the balance of your life?

Most people do not come to a cliff and make the decision to either jump and sell or pull back. They edge into this, usually exploring the possibility of a sale even if they are not really committed to selling. They might engage in this exploration process several times before making the final move. We regard that as constructive since each exploratory process will better educate the owner as to his views about whether or not he really wants to sell.

If, after reading this chapter, you have no further interest in selling your business, you may wish to stop reading here. If you still are interested in selling and wish to explore and understand what's involved, continue reading.

CHAPTER 2

The Preliminaries

If you haven't stopped and put this aside, you are interested in selling your business and want to understand the process. If that is the case, read on!

Finding a Prospective Purchaser

With certain exceptions, no one can find a prospective purchaser better than you can. You know your industry. You may know about others who have sold businesses, and who has purchased them. You probably know whether likely prospects will emerge from competitors, customers, vendors or employees. Sit down, carefully reflect, and try to figure out the likely candidates.

You can contact these prospects directly or use a broker.

Advantages of Using a Broker

Obviously, direct contact is cheaper. However, using a broker can be extremely helpful and is highly recommended. Finding a good broker may be difficult, but is well worth the effort. Selling a business is a very time-consuming task that is likely to become a large distraction from operating your day-to-day business. A good broker will be able to relieve the business owner of much of the burden of the sale process. Moreover, a good broker will help you value your business, identify potential purchasers you may not otherwise be aware of, and prevent you from wasting time with purchasers who are unqualified or just "kicking tires." While you are an expert at operating your business, a broker is an expert at selling a business.

For example, if there will be a solicitation of inquiries from a number of prospective purchasers, a broker will prepare a detailed memorandum summarizing various features of your business: description of business, financial performance, technology, business methods and practices, employees, competitors, etc. Most purchasers do not want to waste time talking to a prospective seller until they have a good overview of the business, although this might not be the case for a purchaser who is knowledgeable about your business.

Putting Your House in Order

Before you launch into the negotiating process, evaluate certain areas and collect your thoughts on the crucial aspects of your business. Below are a few examples of points to consider:

- Make sure you have confidence in the accuracy of your financial statements and income tax returns. A purchaser will expect you to represent that these are correct. Are your financial statements in accordance with Generally Accepted Accounting Principles (GAAP)? If you manipulate your revenues and expenses in a manner that distorts your financial statements, you should anticipate difficulty in persuading a purchaser to restate your financial statements and base the purchase price on the restated statements.

- Do you have any significant contingent liabilities? You will not be able to hide these. It usually is better to present these at an early stage. It is unlikely that you can expect a purchaser to assume these liabilities.

- A purchaser will ask you for your asking price and how you arrived at it. A well-reasoned answer will inspire confidence. You will need to do some careful thinking, and probably discuss this with your broker, accountant and attorney in order to prepare a good response.

- Examine and organize your written agreements, e.g., leases, bank loans, contracts with customers and suppliers, contracts with employees, insurance policies, retirement and employee benefit plans, terms of your customer orders and purchase orders. At some point you will be expected to provide copies and represent that these are enforceable, that no default has occurred, and that the sale and assignment of the contracts is permitted and will not constitute a default.

Professional Advisors

It is unlikely that you can accomplish the above without assistance from an accountant and an attorney who are experienced in these transactions. The most important issues to review are the income tax aspects of the different kinds of transactions, e.g., will it be a purchase of assets or a purchase of stock? You should know and understand the amount of income taxes that will be due and how to minimize these.

Early Contacts With Purchaser

Once a prospective purchaser arrives on the scene, it is impossible to predict the sequence of events. Oftentimes the relative bargaining strength of the parties will dictate the initial meetings and the potential negotiations to follow. If the purchaser is a private equity firm or is offering a premium purchase price, the purchaser in all likelihood will dominate and tell you how to proceed. On the other hand, if you, as the seller, are an exceptionally attractive target for the buyer, you will have leverage to dominate the process. Before proceeding with any exchange of information, the purchaser should sign a Confidentiality Agreement, which is discussed in Chapter 3.

After signing the Confidentiality Agreement, the usual and customary steps are:

- Meet and greet and discuss your business. You will be asked why you have decided to sell. Have a good answer that indicates that you are selling despite your optimism for the future prospects of the business.

- Purchaser will want to see your financial statements.

- Purchaser will want to know your asking price and how you determined this.

CHAPTER 3

Early Stage Documents and Procedures

Confidentiality Agreement (Non-Disclosure Agreement)

At the outset, before delivering any significant information, a seller should insist on a Confidentiality Agreement, often called a Non-Disclosure Agreement (an "NDA"). This usually is a short document that provides that neither party will "use" or "disclose to others" confidential information.

Notwithstanding the clear and prohibitive language of a Confidentiality Agreement, you should be cognizant of its limitations. It is very difficult, and usually impractical, to try to enforce this agreement against a prospective purchaser who you believe may have violated it. The prospective purchaser will claim that the information in question was not confidential and that he did not breach the agreement. Proving a default is very difficult and expensive. Even if you can establish that a default in fact occurred, you will have the vexing problem of proving the monetary value of the damages.

Then what can you do to protect yourself? If the information is secret but not critical to the success of your business, a good example being your financial information, it is highly unlikely that the prospective purchaser will breach his confidentiality undertaking. If he does, just grimace and accept the fact that attempted recourse by you will be futile. On the other hand, for critical secret information, such as the components of a secret formula or special pricing given to large customers or received from major vendors, do not rely on the terms of the Confidentiality Agreement. Exercise the old maxim that possession is 90% of the law. You should make it known to the prospective purchaser that you will not reveal this information until you are ready to do so, and in some cases this might mean no revelation until immediately after the closing. At the early stages, you may choose to withhold names of customers, suppliers and employees, identifying them by code letters or numbers and percentages of business until you are more comfortable with the purchaser and his desire and ability to purchase your business.

Not revealing critical confidential information is particularly important if the prospective purchaser is, or may become, a direct competitor. Although a competitor often is the most likely purchaser and should be given an opportunity to buy your business, it does present very delicate problems and requires a great deal of ingenuity, since the prospective purchaser usually needs information in advance in order to determine his willingness to proceed. At the same time you, as seller, are reluctant to provide information to a competitor. Our experience is that the parties usually find some method for achieving a mutually satisfactory compromise that provides the seller with protection if the deal fails to close. One instance that we recall was a situation where the parties were competitors and did not trust each other. The compromise reached was that the purchaser (our client) put up $1.0 million in escrow that would be paid to the seller if the transaction failed to close. Fortunately, the sale closed.

In most cases, the exchange of confidential information presents no problems, but there are unusual circumstances that require unorthodox solutions in order to make the deal.

Directions to Your Attorney and Accountant

Often the prospective buyer and seller will agree on a price and expect their respective attorneys to easily and quickly proceed to finalize the various documents. However, if you believe that a quick and easy signing and closing will occur, you are being naive, and we would like to talk to you about selling you a very large bridge that transports thousands of autos daily between Brooklyn and Manhattan!

The legal process of documenting a purchase and sale transaction usually is a nightmare to a seller with no prior experience in selling a business. The balance of this book will point out many of the issues that a seller can expect to encounter.

One worthwhile step you can take at the very outset is to give your attorney one of the following specific directions:

- I do not want to take any risks and I would rather have the deal fall through than experience an aftermath of problems; or,

- I very much want to consummate this deal and I am willing to accept a contract that is less than 100% perfect in protecting me.

No matter which of the above instructions you give at the outset, you will have to carefully follow the process and make sure your edict is being faithfully followed. Of course, as the deal progresses, your views on this may change.

Letter of Intent

This is a very important document to the buyer, and the seller should proceed with this even though the binding provisions favor the buyer. Typically, a Letter of Intent is non-binding, except for a provision that prohibits the seller from seeking a sale of his business or negotiating with any other prospective buyer for a period of about 60 - 90 days. The purchaser reasonably needs such a prohibition as he does not want to invest the time and money to pursue the necessary due diligence without the seller's assurance that the seller will deal exclusively with the prospective buyer during this 60 - 90 day period.

Although some may disagree with our view, even if the 60 - 90 day period has expired, we usually recommend that a seller restrict his negotiations with a single prospective purchaser until those negotiations have resulted in a binding contract or have terminated. Simultaneously negotiating with more than one prospective buyer is a big turn-off to a serious buyer, and is likely to dampen his enthusiasm for the deal even in the absence of a restriction in the Letter of Intent. It is reminiscent of the dating process, i.e., it usually is best to date one girl (or one guy) at a time, or if you are dating more than one, make sure you keep it a secret.

At the stage of drafting the Letter of Intent, the buyer and seller usually work out the basics of the anticipated purchase and sale as follows:

       (a)   Price. This is the most critical term of the deal. We address this in greater detail in Chapter 8.

       (b)   Payment. Terms of payment, i.e., all cash at closing or some deferred payments. If there are no deferred payments, the buyer probably will want some of the purchase price placed into an escrow to secure the seller's undertakings in the Purchase Agreement. The size of the escrow is open for negotiations, depending on the financial responsibility of the seller, the number and size of potential problems and numerous other factors. A seller should beware if the buyer insists on too large an escrow, as that might signify that the buyer intends to try to recoup some of the purchase price by making post-closing claims for the seller's breach of provisions in the agreement. A seller should probably make careful inquiry regarding previous acquisitions by the prospective purchaser. Get the names of prior sellers, and discuss with them whether your prospective purchaser was reasonable and upstanding or a bad actor. This might be one of the most important due diligence procedures that you, as seller, can take.

       (c)   Form of Transaction. Whether the form of transaction is a sale of assets or sale of stock is a very important issue. From the seller's perspective a sale of stock yields a much better income tax result. All of the gain will be long-term capital gain. A sale of assets usually results in a portion of the gain being taxed as ordinary income, e.g., depreciation recapture or LIFO inventory recapture. Although a sale of stock is much better tax-wise to the seller, the opposite is true for the buyer. The buyer wants to purchase assets since he can then increase the income tax cost basis of the assets and accelerate his income tax deductions following the purchase. If the form of transaction is a purchase of stock, the buyer will inherit all of the seller's liabilities, but the buyer can avoid succeeding to many of the seller's liabilities if the transaction is structured as an asset purchase.

The income tax problem becomes acute if the seller is a C Corporation as opposed to an S Corporation. The sale of assets of a C Corporation results in a double income tax to the seller, one tax at the corporate level and a second tax on distributions to the shareholders in the form of ordinary or liquidating dividends.

Despite the problems that are presented to the seller from a sale of assets, it is our experience that most transactions involving the sale of privately held corporations are structured as asset sales. Sometimes, however, it is necessary for the seller to sell stock rather than to structure the transaction as a sale of assets. For example, the corporation being sold might have leases, contracts or permits that cannot be assigned without obtaining the consent of the third party, which might be difficult or impossible to obtain.

(d)   Agreements With Seller's Stockholders. Usually the Letter of Intent will describe agreements with the individual owners of the selling corporation that will be effective following the closing.   Examples of these include employment agreements, covenants not to compete and a lease for real estate being retained by the seller or its stockholders.

(e)   Seller's   Representations,   Warranties   and Indemnities. Although the provisions covering seller's representations, warranties and indemnities will occupy as much as 50% - 60% of the language of the final Purchase Agreement, and often will involve meticulous negotiation by the attorneys over every word, virtually always these are briefly and casually addressed in the Letter of Intent. The Letter of Intent will state that the final agreement will contain "representations, warranties and indemnities that are usual and customary" for a similar transaction, even though the lawyers know that there is no such thing as "usual and customary." Such a conclusion is warranted by the fact that it is not practical at the Letter of Intent stage to try to sort out and address the detail contained in these provisions. In the Letter of Intent, the seller might want to try to define some of the limits on indemnification, e.g., that purchaser's rights to be indemnified will expire at some

13

point, or that no indemnification will be necessary unless an individual claim exceeds a threshold amount or the aggregate of all claims exceeds a threshold amount. This will be more fully discussed in Chapter 5.

As previously stated, all of the above provisions will be non-binding, except for the binding provision prohibiting the seller from being in contact with or negotiating with anyone else for a period of 60 - 90 days.

In the course of preparing the Letter of Intent, the buyer and seller will sort out and prepare for various issues that will arise. For example, there may be consents required from governmental agencies, customers, vendors, lessors or others. A Letter of Intent often expresses the parties' intentions as to when they expect to sign a definitive Purchase Agreement and when they expect to close.

Even though most of the terms are not binding, the Letter of Intent is the foundation for the definitive agreement that will follow, and the Letter of Intent should be taken very seriously by the seller. This is the time when the buyer is romancing the seller. Use this as an opportunity to address the matters that you regard as serious and important to you. Do not relax because the Letter of Intent is not binding. This is your best moment, and you should not be lulled into complacency by the thought that you can raise matters of concern later. On the other hand, don't overplay your hand.

CHAPTER 4

Due Diligence

The purchaser will be performing due diligence from the very outset until just before closing. The amount of due diligence will depend on the purchaser's knowledge of your business and the purchaser's business procedures. Although this is a big pain to the seller, and unnecessary from the seller's viewpoint, since the seller already knows the details, it is important to grin and bear it and cooperate fully with the purchaser's requests, within reason.

What is the purchaser trying to achieve in the course of his due diligence? Some of the purchaser's main objectives are:

- First, a general overview of your business. The purchaser will be considering whether he needs to modify some of your methods and procedures.

- Acquiring knowledge of your customers, vendors and employees.

- Purchaser and his accountants will attempt to ascertain whether there are any contractual or other liabilities that purchaser will want to avoid and not assume.

- Purchaser will carefully review your financial statements and determine for himself their accuracy, even though the seller will represent and warrant their accuracy.

- Purchaser will want to confirm that you have adequate insurance coverage, particularly for product liability claims for products delivered and accidents occurring prior to the closing.

- Employee records and benefit plans will be reviewed to determine how your employees will be integrated into the purchaser's plans for compensation and employee benefits. In all likelihood these will differ from your plans.

- Throughout this process the purchaser and his representatives will be looking for specific items that, in purchaser's view, should be addressed in the Purchase Agreement.

The culmination of the due diligence process is the preparation of Schedules that will be attached to and become a part of the Purchase Agreement. Schedules that are attached to and incorporated into the Purchase Agreement differ from Exhibits that also are attached. Exhibits are more fully discussed in Chapter 10.

Typical Schedules may include the following items: listing of customers, suppliers, employees, leases, contracts, insurance policies, retirement plans, pending litigation, consents required and exceptions to Representations and Warranties. Schedules (or Exhibits) might also set forth the allocation of the purchase price and accounting methods and procedures for determining certain items, e.g., working capital to be left in the business and calculations of inventory. You, as the seller, will be asked and required to represent and warrant the correctness of the lists reflected on these Schedules. Therefore, you and your representatives should carefully follow the due diligence process and maintain records and copies of documents and data delivered to the purchaser's representatives since these documents and data constitute the information that will be used in preparing the Schedules that you will be warranting are complete and accurate.

We recommend that early on, no later than when you see the first draft of the Purchase Agreement, you ascertain the Schedules that will be attached to the Purchase Agreement. In this way, your representatives can begin preparing drafts of the Schedules as the due diligence process evolves.

Do not mislead yourself into thinking that if the purchaser acquires knowledge of a problem or potential liability during the due diligence process, this means the purchaser has assumed this and released you from the obligation. That is not how the process works and is not the function of the due diligence process. If purchaser is to undertake an obligation or liability, it must be expressly stated in the Purchase Agreement. For that reason you should use the due diligence process to disclose problems, and then see if you can negotiate with the purchaser some arrangement whereby the purchaser assumes some or all of the problem.

In recent years, sophisticated purchasers, usually private equity firms or others that regularly purchase companies, have started using Electronic Data Rooms ("EDR") as a confidential central repository of due diligence information. The EDR can be uploaded and easily accessed by persons in many locations, eliminating much of the inefficient copying and transmitting of papers that previously took place. Some purchasers may use an EDR only to show their technical proficiency. Even though a purchaser uses an EDR, it is likely that the purchaser also will require you to prepare the Schedules for attachment to the Purchase Agreement.

If your purchaser requires an EDR, you probably will have to go along with that requirement. If you can persuade purchaser not to use an EDR, you may simplify the due diligence process for yourself, and save a substantial amount of professional expense and time of your internal representatives.

Contrary to what one might expect, our experience is that the extensive use of computer technology in the sale of a business has made the process much more complicated and expensive, but we are now in the 21st century and it is impossible to turn back the clock.

CHAPTER 5

The Structure of the Purchase Agreement (PA);
Stock Purchase Agreements (SPA's) and
Asset Purchase Agreements (APA's)

Most Purchase Agreements ("PA's"), whether a Stock Purchase Agreement ("SPA") or an Asset Purchase Agreement ("APA"), have the same structure. The PA usually will have Schedules and Exhibits that are attached to and made a part of the PA.

<u>Introductory Provisions</u>

The first page or so identifies the parties and sets forth a few preambles. The first section often sets forth terms that are defined and used later in the PA, but some prefer to place the defined terms at the end of the PA.

<u>Purchase Price and Payment</u>

After the introduction and definitions, the PA usually sets forth the description of assets (or stock) to be sold, the Purchase Price and the terms of payment. Frequently, the Purchase Price is a formula, based in whole or in part on a level of earnings, sales or net worth (which will be covered in greater detail on Chapter 8). These formulae typically involve detail regarding the accounting procedures to be used and are likely to be described in a Schedule rather than the body of the PA. This Schedule might be the most important part of the PA. Another item frequently covered is the requirement that the business, at closing, retain a minimum amount of working capital.

Liabilities and Obligations

The APA also will delineate the liabilities and obligations that the purchaser will or will not assume. Generally, in an APA, a purchaser will assume none of the seller's liabilities and obligations, other than certain desirable contracts that the purchaser has reviewed and outstanding sales orders and purchase orders.

Seller's Representations and Warranties

The next section of the PA is one that occupies many pages of narrative text, i.e., the Representations and Warranties of the seller. The purchaser will expect the seller to represent and warrant virtually every aspect of the seller's business, e.g.:

- that it is duly organized;

- that the seller has necessary power and authority;

- correctness of seller's financial records, financial statements and income tax returns;

- that the seller's contracts, orders and permits listed are true and complete and not in default;

- description of pending and past litigation;

- representations concerning collectability of accounts receivable, quality of seller's inventory, condition of fixed assets, full payment of taxes and the absence of other liabilities;

- representations concerning compliance with environmental and other laws;

- description of transactions, if any, with related parties;

- description of employee benefit plans and confirmation regarding compliance with laws; and

- that there are no brokers or finders.

As stated earlier, the seller's Representations and Warranties occupy 50% - 60% of the text of the PA. Usually most of the attached detailed Schedules are incorporated into and made part of the Representations and Warranties. Therefore these dominate the time spent by the parties and their attorneys in arriving at mutually agreeable language. However, these are not an end in themselves, but rather the lead-in to the indemnity provisions discussed below. The indemnity provisions are, in our opinion, the most important provisions of the PA. We are not suggesting that the seller's Representations and Warranties should not be seriously addressed, but we are suggesting that a seller can rectify or avoid some of the problems in the Representations and Warranties by careful attention to the indemnity provisions.

Purchaser's Representations and Warranties;
Covenants; Conditions Precedent; Closing

When you get through the seller's Representations and Warranties, you should be finished with about half of the PA. The next few sections usually are:

- purchaser's Representations and Warranties (minimal compared to those of the seller);

- covenants of the seller that largely relate to the preservation of the business in its "ordinary course" between signing and closing plus a few post-closing covenants; and

- conditions precedent that will permit the purchaser or seller to abandon the deal if certain representations, warranties or covenants are breached.

We have found it very helpful to have a "Closing" section that enumerates all of the documents that each of the seller and purchaser will deliver at the closing, including bills of sale, assignments, assumptions and authority documents. By listing all of the documents carefully in the "Closing" section, the terms of these documents can be considered and negotiated simultaneously with the preparation of the PA, thus permitting the closing to be swift and efficient following signing of the PA.

Indemnification by Seller

The seller's indemnity section carefully enumerates all of the matters that will require a seller to indemnify the purchaser for liabilities or risks that the purchaser will not assume, e.g., breach of a representation or warranty, breach of a covenant, a liability or third party claim asserted against the purchaser for which the seller agrees to be responsible, tax liabilities of the seller and other events that occurred prior to closing.

A seller's indemnity is usually broadly stated, but various limitations have become customary as described below:

(a)   Basket or *De Minimis*. If a single claim of the purchaser is below a small amount or if the aggregate of all of the purchaser's claims are below a threshold amount, it is customary that the seller will have no indemnification liability. The theory of this limitation is that the cost of pursuing small claims exceeds the benefit. However, the definition of a small claim and the threshold aggregate amount is by no means uniform.   In trying to evolve a minimum amount or the aggregate amount above which a seller will not be liable for anything, there is a wide range of opinion as to what is "customary and reasonable." When representing purchasers we have encountered seller's attorneys that have asked that the aggregate be 2% to 3% of the purchase price, which we regard as much too high. Our opinion is that about 0.5% to 1% of the purchase price is reasonable, i.e., for a $10 million deal there should be an aggregate threshold of $50,000 to $100,000. Once the aggregate is agreed upon, it then becomes an issue whether the seller should indemnify only for the excess over the aggregate amount, or the seller should indemnify for all claims if the aggregate amount is exceeded. We know of no standard for resolving this, and the decision will turn on which party is willing to make concessions in order to get on with the deal.

(b)   Direct or Consequential Damages. A limitation that we consider very important to the seller is that a seller should be liable only for the purchaser's direct out-of-pocket losses and not consequential damages.   For example, if a purchaser predicated the purchase price on a multiple of earnings, e.g., 7 or 8 times earnings, should a $50,000 claim be measured by the $50,000 out-of-pocket amount, or by a multiple of 7 or 8 times $50,000? A seller should address and cover this in the indemnification section.   "Consequential damages" is a legal theory that, under certain circumstances, extends damages beyond the immediate out-of-pocket loss (to include for example, lost profits). The seller should seek to expressly eliminate consequential damages in the indemnity section.

(c)   Cap on Damages. Often there is a cap or a limit stating that seller's indemnification will not exceed a specified amount. Sometimes the specified amount is the Purchase Price, but sometimes a lower amount is specified. Our experience has been that if a seller negotiates too hard to establish a low limit, it might indicate that the seller is concerned and this often persuades the purchaser to dig in and not accept the seller's proposed limit. The better approach for a seller may be not to seek a low limit, but to seriously address the various provisions so that the seller is confident that any indemnity will be non-existent or minimal in amount.

(d)   Expiration of Indemnity. We recommend trying to establish an outside date after which a purchaser may not give any notice of a claim, i.e., it acts as a statute of limitations. This gives the seller comfort that after some period of time, he can be free of the transaction and no longer have to worry about claims being brought. Sometimes this period is one year after the closing, but three years after the closing is more typical. Our experience has been that it usually is necessary to differentiate the period of limitations for different indemnifications. For example, indemnification for failure to provide good title to the assets (or stock) sold may be open indefinitely.   Indemnification for unpaid taxes or other third party claims should be open until the expiration of the applicable statute of limitations. Thus, the 1 - 3 year limitation period for giving notice of a claim usually will have several exceptions.

(e)   Other Limitations on Seller's Indemnification

(1)   Require the purchaser to give prompt notice of each claim. Otherwise the purchaser can sit on claims and present these all at once if business conditions have deteriorated and the purchaser is dissatisfied with the deal he made.

(2)   Provide that the seller can handle and defend against third party claims at the seller's expense.

(3)   Some attorneys representing sellers try to obtain a limitation that an indemnification will be reduced if the claim reduces the purchaser's income taxes. This is a very difficult provision to negotiate and draft, as indemnification usually will have the effect of reducing the purchase price and will not provide the purchaser with immediate income tax benefits. When representing a seller, we have not generally encouraged this, reasoning that it is better to refrain from trying to obtain something that you ultimately will concede.

Indemnification by Purchaser

Although the PA will provide for indemnification by the purchaser, as a practical matter it is not meaningful. Ordinarily the PA will not even set forth limitations that correspond to the limitations applicable to the seller.

Survival

Subject to the limitations set forth above, the indemnification provisions usually survive the closing date and impose an obligation on the seller to pay the purchaser for any indemnification.

Boilerplate Provisions

Typically there are about 5 or so pages of so-called boilerplate provisions covering the following: no assignment without consent; giving of notice; no oral changes; governing law; each party to pay its own expenses; principles applicable if the PA is terminated; and others.

Dispute Resolution

A very important provision deals with how and where disputes are resolved. Should disputes be litigated in a court and, if the seller and purchaser reside in different jurisdictions, which court? Or should disputes be arbitrated, and if so, where? Do not consider this a boilerplate or meaningless provision. It might be one of the most important provisions of the PA. Litigating or arbitrating in your home jurisdiction could prove an important "home court advantage." Often the parties agree in advance upon an independent accountant to be the final arbiter of accounting disputes.

Exhibits

Typical Exhibits are: an Escrow Agreement; a Lease for real estate owned by the seller and leased to the purchaser; an Employment or Consulting Agreement for the seller's owner or key employees; and a Covenant Not To Compete. These will be discussed in Chapter 10.

CHAPTER 6

The First Draft of the Purchase Agreement;
A Word About Attorneys

If your prospective purchaser is willing to allow you to prepare the first draft of the PA, beware... even if this was prompted by your request to do so. The buyer always wants to, and should, prepare the first draft of the PA since most of the PA is intended to provide necessary disclosures and protection for the buyer. The seller's interest in the PA is more limited: to make sure that the dollar purchase price agreed on will in fact be paid, and to protect against incurring indemnification liabilities to repay the purchaser. If the buyer wants the seller to prepare the first draft of the PA, we doubt that the buyer is serious about pursuing the purchase.

Even before you receive the first draft of the PA, you might want to make some inquiry as to its length. Also, ascertain who the purchaser will use as its counsel. Although you probably cannot do anything to influence these two items, the responses will let you know what to expect in the drafting process.

Hopefully, you will be told that the length of the PA is about 30 to 40 pages, double-spaced, without including Schedules and Exhibits. It also will be reassuring if the buyer tells you that he has instructed his attorney to include the usual provisions that a seller will request in order to shorten the negotiations involved in the drafting process. Shortening the process will reduce your legal expenses, as well as the buyer's legal expenses, which is a very desirable objective.

Unfortunately, most purchasers do not understand that they can achieve all of the necessary protections and achieve all of their objectives through a shorter and well crafted document.

Most first drafts of PA's are more than twice the length of the optimum 30 - 40 double- spaced pages. There usually is a great deal of overkill, and provisions that purchaser's attorney knows the seller's attorney will request are often omitted. Why do attorneys do this? Perhaps it is just their ego, to show their client how smart and tough they are.   Also, protracting the drafting process, although more expensive to the buyer and seller, is more profitable to the attorneys.

In the multitude of transactions in which we have been involved as counsel for the seller, there was only one transaction that we recall when the buyer and its attorney knowingly followed a deliberate shortening of the drafting process. In that instance, the buyer was very familiar with our client's business, and the buyer, over preceding years, acquired many similar businesses and was consolidating these into a large business enterprise. Our client and the buyer had a meeting and agreed on a price. Minimal due diligence was necessary since the price was predicated on a formula, and the buyer was very knowledgeable regarding the business. The buyer's attorney prepared the first draft of about 30 - 40 double-spaced pages. It was a clear and well drafted document. After giving the seller and us several days to review, the buyer's attorney traveled to Chicago, we met, we discussed and agreed on about 10 or so changes of varying degrees of importance, the buyer's attorney entered the language changes into his computer, printed out the revision, and the PA was immediately executed. It was the most efficient process of drafting that we have ever seen or heard of, made possible largely because of the buyer's familiarity with the seller's business. In the numerous transactions where we have represented the purchaser, the only times that we have come close to matching this speed and efficiency were instances when our client, the purchaser, was buying with the intent of immediately liquidating and selling the acquired assets. In those instances, the buyer only had short-term concerns and not the long-term concerns that are typical for a buyer who intends to operate the acquired business indefinitely.

You, as the seller, cannot influence the purchaser's selection of his attorney. You can only hope that his attorney's objective is to make the deal finish rapidly, and that he is not trying to show everyone how smart he is.

But you, as seller, do have control over the selection of your attorney. Ideally, you already have an attorney that you have used on multiple occasions and that you know to be experienced, competent and practical. If that is not the case, you will have to proceed with the necessary due diligence to select a qualified attorney to represent you. Although there are many experienced attorneys that are very knowledgeable in selling a business, it is virtually impossible from a single meeting to determine those who are practical and know how to make a deal happen and those who are unable to quickly distinguish the important features of the deal from those that are remote, unlikely and unimportant.

Do not mislead yourself by seeking someone who is regarded as a "tough" attorney. The best attorney negotiator that we ever encountered, we are proud to say, was our mentor. His style was amazing. In negotiating the detailed provisions of the PA, irrespective of whether he represented the buyer or seller, he would quickly concede every request by the other side that he regarded as reasonable or unimportant to his client. By doing so, he established an environment such that, when he failed to concede a point, the other side knew he was serious, and they usually accepted his view. He had enormous self-confidence in distinguishing between the items that were important to his client and those that were not.

Whether you end up with a first draft of 30 - 40 double-spaced pages or one that is more than twice that length, you and your attorney will likely have a lot of work to do, since there will be numerous Schedules that you will need to prepare identifying all of the contracts, permits, employee retirement and benefit plans, insurance policies, customer orders, purchase orders and other relevant details. The Schedules and the language of the PA will need to be coordinated. Much of the language of the first draft of the PA will need to be qualified to set forth exceptions.

The first draft of the PA is an important starting point. For your sake, we hope that the buyer and the buyer's attorney will present you with a reasonably fair and well-drafted first draft of the PA.

CHAPTER 7

What To Do Following Receipt of the First Draft of the Purchase Agreement (PA)

After receiving and reviewing the first draft of the PA from the buyer, for the first time you will be in a position to determine how long this process will take and whether the sale is likely to consummate or abort.

You will need to analyze the buyer's draft of the PA and formulate an answer to the following questions:

- Are there significant financial and business differences between you and the buyer?

- Is the language of the agreement clear and understandable, or are there many ambiguities?

Assuming that there are significant business and financial issues as well as language ambiguities, the procedure that many attorneys for the seller will follow is to make all of the revisions that he deems reasonable and to send a revised so-called "red-lined draft," i.e., one marked to show changes from the first draft of the PA, to the buyer and the buyer's attorney.

Sometimes the buyer's and seller's attorneys go back and forth with red-lined drafts. often reinserting provisions that the other attorney deleted. This process of multiple exchanges of red-lined drafts often will proceed *ad nauseam* with very little progress being made towards completion.

Depending on the circumstances, we often recommend that instead of a multitude of exchanges of red-lined drafts, the seller and his attorney prepare a "list of outstanding issues." The issues listed can address financial issues as well as ambiguous language. The parties and their attorneys can then proceed with a discussion towards a mutually acceptable resolution of all, or at least many, of the open issues.

Our preference always has been to try to discuss the issues before sending multiple red-lined drafts back and forth. But each transaction is different, and there is no set rule as to how many red-lined drafts are exchanged. Sometimes in the latter stages of completing the PA prior to signing, the attorneys will exchange several red-lined drafts, but often these will merely deal with three or four areas that either arose late in the drafting process or where the language is particularly difficult to resolve.

CHAPTER 8

Special Problems and Issues

This Chapter will only address a few of the multitude of special problems and issues that might arise in the sale of a business. It would be impossible for us to address all of the special problems and issues, and therefore we have selected a few of the more common ones that sellers will confront.

Determining the Purchase Price

Obviously, from the seller's perspective, this is the most important feature of the transaction. Although it has become somewhat standard for private equity firms and sophisticated buyers to determine a purchase price based on a multiple (generally 6 to 8 times) of EBITDA (Earnings Before Interest, Taxes, Depreciation and Amortization), this standard is subject to so many exceptions that it has been relegated to merely one means of determining a purchase price, rather than the only means.

There are many qualified appraisers that value a business based on different approaches, e.g., a multiple of income over trailing 12 months; a market approach that compares the business to publicly held companies with a reduction for non-marketability; and cost or book value with appropriate adjustments. Although business appraisals are commonly used to value a business for tax purposes, these are rarely used by a potential buyer and seller in determining the purchase price, usually because of the time delay involved in obtaining the appraisal and also the variations that an appraiser can achieve depending on the instructions given to him. Potential buyers usually will not be influenced by an appraisal. They will rely on their knowledge and the procedures followed in prior acquisitions in determining the purchase price.   However, despite this, a prospective seller, who has no knowledge of what constitutes a reasonable purchase price, might find it helpful to obtain an appraisal that he can present to a purchaser to assist in obtaining an agreement concerning the purchase price. A seller should anticipate that a qualified appraisal will take about 3 - 4 months and cost upwards of $15,000 depending on the size and complexity of the business being appraised.

Many industries, particularly those with high gross profit margins and those that spend large sums on advertising or marketing that can distort earnings, have developed formulae for measuring the purchase price. For example, in the personal care-consumer products industry, a business often is valued based on a multiple of annual sales, usually 1 to 1½ times. Similarly, in the security alarm business the purchase price is measured by the MRR (monthly recurring revenue) multiplied by a multiplier that might range from 20 to 40 times the MRR. For investment advisers, a purchase price often is based on a multiple of annual net income (excluding the compensation of the owner), but the multiple used might vary from 3 to 10 times. Even when a standard has developed for an industry based on sales or net income, the multipliers used vary greatly and also change from time to time based on business conditions and the number of prospective purchasers seeking to buy companies in that industry.

Service groups, e.g., medical and dental practices and accounting firms, are subject to different measurement standards than other businesses. The measurement of the purchase price is different for a manufacturer, wholesaler or retailer. The buyer and the seller need to carefully investigate the applicable standards that prevail in the seller's industry. If they do so reasonably, they usually will be able to find a mutually agreeable purchase price.

Earnest Money

Although virtually every real estate transaction requires the purchaser to deposit earnest money, this is relatively uncommon in transactions involving the sale of a business. Perhaps the rationale for this is that both the buyer and seller are investing time and money in pursuit of the sale transaction. Alternatively, the reasoning might be that the seller's agreement to refrain from seeking another buyer for

60 - 90 days is not a serious problem for the seller to endure, whereas taking a parcel of real estate off the market for even a short time might be detrimental. Or maybe it is just a custom without an underlying rationale! Also, in most cases the period between signing the PA and closing is very close, i.e., a week or less, and therefore no earnest money need be deposited. It is very difficult for the seller to obtain a deposit of earnest money by the purchaser in advance of signing the PA, but it is something to be considered, particularly if there is doubt about the purchaser's financial capacity to consummate the purchase. If, after signing the PA, there will be an extended period of more than 1 - 2 weeks between signing and closing, we believe that it is reasonable to ask the purchaser to deposit earnest money with an independent escrowee.

Somewhat related to the earnest money issue, and probably more important, is that at the very outset the seller should inquire regarding the purchaser's financial capacity to consummate the purchase. Will the purchaser have to borrow the necessary funds? If so, from whom does he intend to borrow and when will he have a commitment from the lender? It is not unreasonable, but it is not conventional, for a seller to ask that the purchaser put up earnest money that will be forfeited if the purchaser is unable to obtain the necessary financing.

Earn-Out

A buyer and seller, in attempting to find a way to resolve a difference as to the purchase price, often will gravitate to a so-called "earn-out," which is a contingent amount that is predicated on the seller's business achieving a certain level of net income in the 2 - 5 years following the closing. To us, this generally is a recipe for disaster, although we have seen it work out favorably for a seller in several recent cases. The problems arise in two distinct areas:

- There needs to be precise clarity in the PA as to the accounting principles to be followed in calculating the net income earn-out, since frequently the buyer and seller will not account in the same way for many items that go into the calculation of net income.

- The PA needs to express the degree of control that the seller will have over the business's operations even though the business will be owned by the buyer.

If you head in the direction of an earn-out based on net income, you should expect great difficulty in drafting mutually satisfactory provisions regarding the accounting for net income and the seller's desire to control the business operations during the earn-out period. The accounting provisions can be greatly simplified, and the seller will receive greater protection, if the earn-out is based upon net sales or gross profit rather than net income.

<u>Stock Purchases Treated as Asset Acquisitions – Section 338(h)(10)</u>

As previously discussed, the selling corporation may have leases, contracts or permits that cannot be transferred without the consent of a third party whose consent might be difficult or impossible to obtain. Section 338(h)(10) of the Internal Revenue Code (the "Code") provides a means available to certain corporations, i.e., a subsidiary of a consolidated group of corporations or an S Corporation, that will permit a sale of stock to be treated for federal income tax purposes as a sale of assets of the selling corporation. Thus, Section 338(h)(10) creates a fictional sale of assets that is different from the actual form of the sale of stock. For federal income tax purposes, by making the Section 338(h)(10) election, the transaction is transformed into a sale of assets by the selling corporation followed by a liquidation of the selling corporation. If the selling corporation is an S Corporation, the overall tax result usually is a single tax based on the excess of the amount realized on the sale over the selling corporation's basis for the assets sold.

From the viewpoint of the seller, he will prefer that the sale of stock not be transformed into a sale of assets, but the purchaser derives significant income tax benefits from a sale of assets, and this will drive the use of Section 338(h)(10). The election to use Section 338(h)(10) must be made jointly by the seller and purchaser.

The non-tax considerations described in the first sentence of this section are the crucial elements that will cause the parties to proceed with the transaction as a sale of stock and make a Section

338(h)(10) election in order to report it as a sale of assets for federal income tax purposes.

Allocation of Purchase Price

The allocation of the purchase price in a transaction involving the purchase of assets is an important decision affecting income taxes of both seller and buyer. The buyer will want to allocate as much of the purchase price as the buyer can justify to inventory and machinery and equipment since these assets will be deducted more rapidly under the buyer's income tax reporting. However, allocation of purchase price to inventory and machinery and equipment is likely to create ordinary income to the seller from LIFO recapture and depreciation recapture. The seller will usually want to allocate more of the purchase price to items that will result in capital gain to the seller, e.g. intangible property (licenses, patents and trademarks), goodwill and a covenant not to compete. These items, however, can only be deducted by the buyer's amortizing these over 15 years. Thus, the Internal Revenue Service ("IRS") regulations have cleverly created a structure that imposes on the buyer and the seller the obligation to file reports of their asset allocations. Thus, seller and buyer must either agree on an allocation or face the prospect that the IRS will throw both of them into an income tax controversy and let them fight it out to establish the correct allocation of the purchase price.

Most APA's, or SPA's for which a Section 338(h)(10) election is made, contain provisions whereby the buyer and seller agree on the allocation of the purchase price among the acquired assets.

Net Operating Losses and Other Tax Benefits

A detailed review of this area would require a separate book of about the same length as this one. Therefore this subject will receive brief comments and not a detailed review.

This subject can be important in certain circumstances. The seller might have net operating losses, capital losses, tax credits and other beneficial items that can be carried forward or back to reduce taxable income. Similarly, the purchasing corporation might possess such items that can be effectively offset against taxable income generated by the selling corporation.

The utilization of the seller's net operating losses by the purchaser will not carry over to the purchaser if the form of the transaction is a sale of assets. In order for a purchaser to be able to utilize the seller's net operating losses, the transaction must be structured as a sale of stock or a merger, but it also is necessary to circumvent specific provisions of the Code that are intended to prohibit "trafficking in losses" between a seller and buyer.

The statutory limitations imposed by the Code on the transfer of the seller's net operating losses are formidable and difficult to circumvent in a situation in which a closely held corporation wants to be paid a stipend for conveying these to a purchaser. The primary limitation is found in Section 382 of the Code that prevents the purchaser from using the seller's net operating losses if there has been change of ownership of the corporation, i.e., more than a 50% change in value of the loss corporation's stock over a three-year period. Other numerous technical features of Section 382 will not be addressed here.

If the parties can somehow circumvent Section 382 of the Code, they still must deal with Section 269 that disallows deductions and other tax benefits if the principal purpose of the acquisition is to secure tax benefits that the purchaser would not otherwise enjoy.

As a practical matter, a seller should not mislead himself into believing that he can cash in and receive any significant monetary payment for existing net operating losses. A seller's best practice for realizing any monetary value from net operating losses is to elect to be an S Corporation before the losses occur and to offset these losses against other income realized by the S Corporation's shareholders.

Golden Parachute Payments

Sections 280G and 4999 of the Code set forth certain additional taxes and penalties that will arise if "golden parachute payments" are made to key employees. These provisions were enacted to impede the seller's management from consummating a sale in exchange for lucrative employment contracts and severance payments to the managing employees. In general, these provisions deny the paying party a deduction for an excess parachute payment and impose a 20% non-deductible excise tax on the recipient of an "excess parachute payment." An "excess parachute payment" is a payment in connection with a "change of control" that equals or exceeds three times the recipient's average annual compensation for the five prior years.

Fortunately, the Code sets forth several important exceptions that in most instances will render this subject moot. The significant exceptions that make the above Code provisions inapplicable are:

- Any payment made by a corporation (i.e., the buyer or seller) that will meet the general eligibility requirements of an S Corporation (i.e., the paying entity has fewer than 100 shareholders) will not be treated as a parachute payment.

- Any payments made by a corporation that has no publicly traded stock will not be treated as a parachute payment.

- Any payment that is established to be reasonable compensation for services rendered after the change of control will not be treated as a parachute payment.

The issue of "golden parachute payments" rarely arises in the typical acquisition of a privately held business.

Tax-Free Reorganizations and Deferred Payments

Back in the 20th century, tax-free reorganizations were in vogue, and publicly held corporations frequently purchased privately held corporations using stock as the means of paying the purchase price. The seller could receive the publicly traded stock of the acquiring corporation without realizing any taxable gain until the stock was sold.

Now, in the 21st century, this form of transaction is not commonly used, but it still occurs. A purchase for cash, rather than payment in the form of the purchaser's stock, is the more customary form of transaction. Some of the reasons for the shift may be:

- Greater availability of cash that can be accessed through banks and other lenders, private equity funds, venture capital funds and investors.

- Greater awareness by sellers of the risks of holding the stock of the buyer in a declining market.

- The inability of the acquiring corporation to write up the tax basis of the assets of the selling corporation.

- New principles of accounting that were promulgated in 2001 that require the acquiring corporation to follow more restrictive accounting, the effect of which is to reduce the purchaser's reportable net income below what previously was possible under the "pooling of interests" concept that was commonly used prior to 2001.

Before embarking on a tax-free reorganization, a seller should either make a decision himself or engage someone to assist him in evaluating the risks of taking the publicly traded stock of the purchaser rather than cash. It would be presumptuous for us to try to evaluate the economic differences between a taxable sale for cash and a non-taxable sale for stock, since those are investment decisions that should not be addressed by attorneys.

Rather than accepting an all-cash payment of the purchase price at closing, a seller might also consider taking the purchaser's promissory note that spreads out payment over several years. Using the installment method of reporting the gain over several years might result in a lower income tax than reporting the entire gain in the year of the sale. This also is an investment decision that we defer to the seller and his investment advisor.

Environmental Conditions

Often one of the most vexing problems that confronts the buyer and seller is the resolution of the contractual provisions dealing with environmental conditions. Where the sale involves the transfer of title to real estate that might have been exposed to hazardous substances, the magnitude of the problem increases. In some states, like Connecticut, the mere sale of the business, even if the real estate is retained by the seller, can trigger environmental investigation and reporting considerations. The usual procedure to resolve this is to order a Phase I environmental investigation. Should the buyer or seller pay for this? What if the Phase I results are inconclusive, as is frequently the case, and the consultants recommend a Phase II environmental investigation? Should the seller proceed with a Phase II investigation in light of the existence of statutory requirements in most states that everyone (i.e., seller, buyer or consultant) becoming aware of a hazardous contamination is legally obligated to report this to the state Environmental Protection Agency ("EPA")? A potential seller might find himself in the terrible predicament that the sale of his business aborts, but he is left with obligations enforced by the EPA to clean up his property, a situation that would not have occurred at this time had he not gone ahead with the testing required by the buyer.

We know of no usual and customary solution to the problem of testing for and allocating responsibility for contamination and hazardous conditions. We strongly recommend that, before getting bogged down in the multitude of other issues and the minutiae involved in the proposed sale, you should address and resolve the environmental issue. In our experience, this issue, more than any other single issue in the sale transaction, is the cause of the failure of the buyer and seller to consummate the sale. The reason for this is the unknown outer limits of the costs of investigating and remediating environmental conditions. We have witnessed situations where the parties terminated, or seriously considered terminating, a transaction even though the parties, in good faith, believed there were no serious environmental conditions. Although they believed this was the case, they were not certain, and this uncertainty created possible problems at an unacceptably high dollar risk level. We, as attorneys, must be prepared to exercise a high level of ingenuity and diplomacy (particularly when our client is the seller) in addressing environmental problems.

CHAPTER 9

Several Specific Statutory Requirements

Hart-Scott-Rodino

If the Hart-Scott-Rodino Antitrust Improvements Act of 1976, as amended (the "HSR Act") is applicable to your sale, the purchaser and the seller must each submit filings, and there is a mandatory waiting period before the transaction can be closed. The HSR Act only applies if the size of the transaction exceeds $50 million, but there are complex exclusions and exemptions that might remove a $50 million transaction from the reporting and filing requirements of the HSR Act.

For transactions subject to the HSR Act, filings must be made with the Federal Trade Commission ("FTC") and the Department of Justice ("DOJ"). These agencies examine the transaction's likely effects on competition. Usually the waiting period will expire in 30 days, but it is possible to request an early termination. However, unless there are compelling reasons in favor of granting an early termination, it generally will not be allowed. The agencies can extend the 30-day waiting period another 30 days by requesting additional information. It is incumbent on either the FTC or DOJ to initiate an action prior to expiration of the waiting period if it wants to challenge and enjoin the proposed sale.

In today's climate, neither the FTC nor DOJ is likely to challenge any of the smaller transactions within the scope of the HSR Act, absent unusual anti-competitive circumstances. The usual result of the smaller transactions that fall under the HSR Act is that the parties are required to pay a filing fee ranging from $45,000 (for transactions of more than $50 million but less than $100 million) to $280,000 (for transactions of more than $500 million), and each side will incur substantial legal fees in order to compile and submit the detailed information called for under the HSR Act from both purchaser and seller. The applicable waiting period does not begin until the documents are filed and the fee is paid.

Sale to a Foreign-Controlled Entity

A seller that proposes to sell to a purchaser that is owned or controlled by a foreign company may need to consider the following:

- The Committee on Foreign Investment in the United States ("CFIUS") should be notified of the proposed transaction and has 30 days to review the national security and economic implications of the foreign ownership. CFIUS has scrutinized sales of advanced computers, oil interests and ownership of ports to foreign interests and may review transactions with United States allies as well as known enemies. The vast majority of transactions submitted to CFIUS are approved without proceeding with the investigation that CFIUS is authorized to initiate.

- International Traffic in Arms Regulations ("ITAR") controls the import and export of defense-related articles, services and munitions. The goal of ITAR is to prevent the disclosure or transfer of sensitive information to a foreign entity. Companies that are subject to ITAR must report an acquisition by a foreign entity to the U.S. State Department. ITAR companies are required to notify the State Department at least 60 days prior to a transaction's closing.

Bulk Sales Statutes

At one time virtually every state had a so-called "bulk sales statute" requiring that notification of a proposed sale of assets be given to every creditor. There also were other restrictions. Bulk sales statutes frequently required establishing an escrow sufficient in amount to pay all of the creditors. The failure to comply with the bulk sales statute caused the buyer to be liable for the seller's liabilities and obligations, including taxes, if these were not paid by the seller. The bulk sales statutes were so impractical that in most transactions, the buyer normally would accept the seller's agreement to indemnify the buyer for the failure to comply with the bulk sales statute. If the buyer had concerns about the seller's financial ability to pay its obligations and liabilities or its undertaking to indemnify the buyer, the parties could set aside funds in an escrow to back up the seller's agreements. Most states, including Illinois, have now repealed these bulk sales statutes, but it is important to verify whether there is a state bulk sales statute applicable to your transaction.

Although Illinois has repealed its bulk sales statute, it has another statute, called a "bulk sales clearance" statute, that renders a buyer liable for the seller's unpaid Illinois income, sales and employment taxes (but not other liabilities) unless the parties give advance notice to the Illinois Department of Revenue ("IDR") and Illinois Department of Employment Security ("IDES"). Upon receiving notice, the IDR and IDES will give the parties notice of an amount to be withheld to satisfy any unpaid Illinois taxes. In a sale of assets, in Illinois, it is customary to request a "bulk sales clearance" from the IDR and IDES and to comply with the terms of the notice by withholding or placing in escrow the amount of Illinois taxes estimated by the IDR and IDES to be due from the seller. It can take 20 - 30 days following submission to the IDR and IDES to receive a notice of the amount to be withheld for estimated unpaid taxes.

WARN Act

If more than 50 full time employees will lose their jobs within a 90-day period as a result of the sale, then the Worker Adjustment and Retraining Notification Act ("WARN Act") may be triggered. Under the WARN Act, if the sale of a business results in a "mass layoff" or "plant closing," the employer must provide 60 days advance notice to all affected employees and any applicable unions and governmental entities. Illinois and many other states have similar statutes. If the seller meets these thresholds, it will be important to determine whether the WARN Act applies and how the parties intend to comply with its provisions.

A Plan to Circumvent Illinois Taxes Imposed On An S Corporation

The Illinois income tax imposed on the gain realized by an S Corporation on the sale of substantially all of its assets is 2.5%. Thus, on a gain of $10 million, the Illinois tax would be $250,000.

Within the last several years, a colleague told us of a plan that he knew for circumventing these taxes. The plan involved minor modifications to the form of the transaction. Before he told us of this, he extracted our pledge that, although we could use the plan, we would not communicate this to others. Therefore, although we cannot reveal any details, we are permitted to state that there is a method of avoiding these Illinois taxes on the gain realized by an S Corporation on the sale of substantially all of its assets.

CHAPTER 10

The Exhibits to the Purchase Agreement

Escrow Agreement

As discussed above, escrows are frequently established to hold a portion of the purchase price for a certain period in order to reimburse the purchaser for liabilities and indemnification obligations of seller. An Escrow Agreement usually is included as an Exhibit. At closing it is executed to set forth the rules for the disbursing of funds from the escrow. The terms of the Escrow Agreement are straightforward. On specified dates, funds will be distributed to the seller unless the purchaser notifies the escrowee of existing claims. If the escrowee receives such notice, the escrowee will continue to hold the funds until the escrowee receives either (1) a joint direction signed by both buyer and seller, or (2) a valid final decree of a court or arbitral tribunal. At the end of the escrow period, if there are no existing claims by the buyer, the remaining funds will be disbursed to the seller.

Covenant Not To Compete

This is one of the more critical features of the sale of a business. No purchaser wants to purchase a business, only to find the seller or its owners competing directly against the buyer. Although many attorneys draft the Covenant Not To Compete as part of the body of the PA, we prefer to handle this as an Exhibit, irrespective of whether we are representing the seller or buyer. Our rationale for this is not to further protract the length of the PA and, in the event of a breach of the Covenant Not To Compete, to have a separate agreement that is focused only on that particular issue, and not burdened by many pages of other language in the PA. Also, the seller might be a corporation, in which case the corporation is the signer of the PA, but a Covenant Not To Compete generally will be signed by the seller and the key individuals who operate the business of the seller. Most of the language of the Covenant Not To Compete is boilerplate. Below are several areas that comprise the essential features:

- <u>Term</u>. Obviously, the seller wants the non-competition term to be as short as possible, but the seller should very cautiously approach how he reveals his thinking to the buyer since it is possible to alarm the buyer. This could impel the buyer to gravitate to a longer term than he otherwise would have accepted. Since the term of a non-competition covenant is not legally enforceable if it exceeds a reasonable term, most buyers request a term of 5 years which is generally considered to be enforceable. If a seller resists and requests 3 years, the buyer may be on notice that you might harbor secret intentions of returning to this business as a competitor. Several times when we encountered this in the course of representing the buyer, our client (the buyer) insisted on asking for a term of 10 years even though he previously might have been willing to accept 5 years. Since the provisions of the covenant provide that the term is automatically reduced to whatever term is legally enforceable, the buyer is not prejudiced by requesting a term beyond what is legally enforceable. The seller is put in a position that he might have to undergo a lawsuit, with all of the expense and uncertainty, if he wants to challenge the legal enforceability of the term of 10 years.

- <u>Area</u>. The area covered by the non-competition covenant also must be reasonable in order to be legally enforceable, and therefore it should be restricted to the territory in which the seller previously conducted business and possibly to the area in which it is reasonably expected that business will be conducted in the future. This ordinarily presents little or no difficulty for the parties to resolve.

- <u>Non-Solicitation of Customers, Vendors or Employees</u>. A buyer customarily will request, and a seller should probably agree, that the seller will not solicit customers, vendors or employees that will in any way, directly or indirectly, be detrimental to the buyer.

Since some states have enacted statutes that define what constitutes a valid term and area of a non-competition agreement, make sure this is considered and researched.

<u>Other Exhibits</u>

The other Exhibits that frequently are attached to a PA are an Employment or Consulting Contract for the owner or key employees and a Lease for real estate that is omitted from the sale, but is being leased to the buyer. Since these documents probably are familiar to most of you and since these are so individually tailored, these will not be further discussed here.

CONCLUSION

Each business is unique, and every sale of a business is a unique experience. The personalities and experience of each buyer, seller and their representatives shape the transaction, and each of these individuals is totally different from parties previously encountered. Trial lawyers encounter this daily. No two juries are the same. The same is true for the individuals you are dealing with in a sale of business transaction. In the course of a transaction involving the sale of a business and the long contractual documents involved, it usually takes a little time for the parties and their representatives to adjust to and get comfortable with each other and their documents. Often a contractual provision initially considered to be unacceptable by the seller becomes acceptable as further thought is given or if some minor modification is made.

Selling a business is both an art and a science. There are a host of technical features and considerations, but the critical parts of the transaction often are decided based on feelings and instinct. Thus, we, as counsel, and our client, as the seller, working together, hopefully can be a combination of Rembrandt and Einstein. We are not suggesting that the successful consummation of the sale of a business is comparable to the magnificent accomplishments of these two geniuses. Rather, we suggest that the qualities needed to accomplish the sought-after result are the exercise of patience, pragmatism and perseverance combined with years of business experience... and perhaps just a dash of creativity.

Printed in Great Britain
by Amazon